2022-2023
18 Month Planner
Weekly & Monthly

Thank you so much for choosing our planners.
Please don't hesitate to leave us a rating or review.

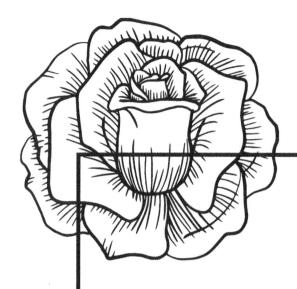
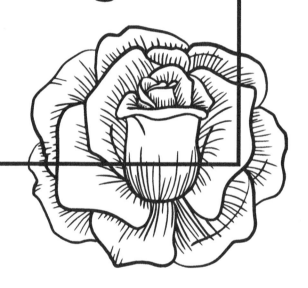

This planner belongs to:

PERSONAL INFORMATION

Name: ....

Address: ....

City: .... State: ....

Phone: ....

Email: ....

Emergency contacts

Name: .... Name: ....

Relationship: .... Relationship: ....

Phone: .... Phone: ....

Email: .... Email: ....

Doctor: .... Doctor: ....

Phone: .... Phone: ....

Email: .... Email: ....

Other

....

....

....

....

CONTACTS

Name:

Address:

Phone:

Email:

Name:

Address:

Phone:

Email:

Name:

Address:

Phone:

Email:

Name:

Address:

Phone:

Email:

Name:

Address:

Phone:

Email:

Name:

Address:

Phone:

Email:

Name:

Address:

Phone:

Email:

Name:

Address:

Phone:

Email:

CONTACTS

Name:

Address:

Phone:

Email:

Name:

Address:

Phone:

Email:

Name:

Address:

Phone:

Email:

Name:

Address:

Phone:

Email:

Name:

Address:

Phone:

Email:

Name:

Address:

Phone:

Email:

Name:

Address:

Phone:

Email:

Name:

Address:

Phone:

Email:

PASSWORD LOG

Website: --

Username: --

Password: --

Notes: --

Website: --

Username: --

Password: --

Notes: --

Website: --

Username: --

Password: --

Notes: --

Website: --

Username: --

Password: --

Notes: --

Website: --

Username: --

Password: --

Notes: --

Website: --

Username: --

Password: --

Notes: --

Website: --

Username: --

Password: --

Notes: --

Website: --

Username: --

Password: --

Notes: --

PASSWORD LOG

Website: --

Username: --

Password: --

Notes: --

Website: --

Username: --

Password: --

Notes: --

Website: --

Username: --

Password: --

Notes: --

Website: --

Username: --

Password: --

Notes: --

Website: --

Username: --

Password: --

Notes: --

Website: --

Username: --

Password: --

Notes: --

Website: --

Username: --

Password: --

Notes: --

Website: --

Username: --

Password: --

Notes: --

2022

January

M	T	W	Th	F	S	Su
					1	2
3	4	5	6	7	8	9
10	11	12	13	14	15	16
17	18	19	20	21	22	23
24	25	26	27	28	29	30
31						

February

M	T	W	Th	F	S	Su
	1	2	3	4	5	6
7	8	9	10	11	12	13
14	15	16	17	18	19	20
21	22	23	24	25	26	27
28						

March

M	T	W	Th	F	S	Su
	1	2	3	4	5	6
7	8	9	10	11	12	13
14	15	16	17	18	19	20
21	22	23	24	25	26	27
28	29	30	31			

April

M	T	W	Th	F	S	Su
				1	2	3
4	5	6	7	8	9	10
11	12	13	14	15	16	17
18	19	20	21	22	23	24
25	26	27	28	29	30	

May

M	T	W	Th	F	S	Su
						1
2	3	4	5	6	7	8
9	10	11	12	13	14	15
16	17	18	19	20	21	22
23	24	25	26	27	28	29
30	31					

June

M	T	W	Th	F	S	Su
		1	2	3	4	5
6	7	8	9	10	11	12
13	14	15	16	17	18	19
20	21	22	23	24	25	26
27	28	29	30			

July

M	T	W	Th	F	S	Su
				1	2	3
4	5	6	7	8	9	10
11	12	13	14	15	16	17
18	19	20	21	22	23	24
25	26	27	28	29	30	31

August

M	T	W	Th	F	S	Su
1	2	3	4	5	6	7
8	9	10	11	12	13	14
15	16	17	18	19	20	21
22	23	24	25	26	27	28
29	30	31				

September

M	T	W	Th	F	S	Su
			1	2	3	4
5	6	7	8	9	10	11
12	13	14	15	16	17	18
19	20	21	22	23	24	25
26	27	28	29	30		

October

M	T	W	Th	F	S	Su
					1	2
3	4	5	6	7	8	9
10	11	12	13	14	15	16
17	18	19	20	21	22	23
24	25	26	27	28	29	30
31						

November

M	T	W	Th	F	S	Su
	1	2	3	4	5	6
7	8	9	10	11	12	13
14	15	16	17	18	19	20
21	22	23	24	25	26	27
28	29	30				

December

M	T	W	Th	F	S	Su
			1	2	3	4
5	6	7	8	9	10	11
12	13	14	15	16	17	18
19	20	21	22	23	24	25
26	27	28	29	30	31	

2023

January

M	T	W	Th	F	S	Su
						1
2	3	4	5	6	7	8
9	10	11	12	13	14	15
16	17	18	19	20	21	22
23	24	25	26	27	28	29
30	31					

February

M	T	W	Th	F	S	Su
		1	2	3	4	5
6	7	8	9	10	11	12
13	14	15	16	17	18	19
20	21	22	23	24	25	26
27	28					

March

M	T	W	Th	F	S	Su
		1	2	3	4	5
6	7	8	9	10	11	12
13	14	15	16	17	18	19
20	21	22	23	24	25	26
27	28	29	30	31		

April

M	T	W	Th	F	S	Su
					1	2
3	4	5	6	7	8	9
10	11	12	13	14	15	16
17	18	19	20	21	22	23
24	25	26	27	28	29	30

May

M	T	W	Th	F	S	Su
1	2	3	4	5	6	7
8	9	10	11	12	13	14
15	16	17	18	19	20	21
22	23	24	25	26	27	28
29	30	31				

June

M	T	W	Th	F	S	Su
			1	2	3	4
5	6	7	8	9	10	11
12	13	14	15	16	17	18
19	20	21	22	23	24	25
26	27	28	29	30		

July

M	T	W	Th	F	S	Su
					1	2
3	4	5	6	7	8	9
10	11	12	13	14	15	16
17	18	19	20	21	22	23
24	25	26	27	28	29	30
31						

August

M	T	W	Th	F	S	Su
	1	2	3	4	5	6
7	8	9	10	11	12	13
14	15	16	17	18	19	20
21	22	23	24	25	26	27
28	29	30	31			

September

M	T	W	Th	F	S	Su
				1	2	3
4	5	6	7	8	9	10
11	12	13	14	15	16	17
18	19	20	21	22	23	24
25	26	27	28	29	30	

October

M	T	W	Th	F	S	Su
						1
2	3	4	5	6	7	8
9	10	11	12	13	14	15
16	17	18	19	20	21	22
23	24	25	26	27	28	29
30	31					

November

M	T	W	Th	F	S	Su
		1	2	3	4	5
6	7	8	9	10	11	12
13	14	15	16	17	18	19
20	21	22	23	24	25	26
27	28	29	30			

December

M	T	W	Th	F	S	Su
				1	2	3
4	5	6	7	8	9	10
11	12	13	14	15	16	17
18	19	20	21	22	23	24
25	26	27	28	29	30	31

HOLIDAYS 2022

HOLIDAY	DAY	PUBLIC HOLIDAY
New year's day	Jan. 1	Friday, Dec. 31
Martin Luther King Jr. Day	Third Monday in January	Monday, Jan. 17
Washington's Birthday	Third Monday in February	Monday, Feb. 21
Memorial Day	Last Monday in May	Monday, May 30
Juneteenth	June 19	Monday, June 20
Independence Day	July 4	Monday, July 4
Labor Day	First Monday in September	Monday, Sept. 5
Columbus Day	Second Monday in October	Monday, Oct. 10
Veterans Day	Nov. 11	Friday, Nov. 11
Thanksgiving Day	Fourth Thursday in November	Thursday, Nov. 24
Christmas Day	Dec. 25	Monday, Dec. 26

HOLIDAYS 2023

HOLIDAY	DAY	PUBLIC HOLIDAY
New year's day	Jan. 1	Monday, Jan. 02
Martin Luther King Jr. Day	Third Monday in January	Monday, Jan. 16
Washington's Birthday	Third Monday in February	Monday, Feb. 20
Memorial Day	Last Monday in May	Monday, May 29
Juneteenth	June 19	Monday, June 19
Independence Day	July 4	Tuesday, July 4
Labor Day	First Monday in September	Monday, Sept. 4
Columbus Day	Second Monday in October	Monday, Oct. 9
Veterans Day	Nov. 11	Saturday, Nov. 11
Thanksgiving Day	Fourth Thursday in November	Thursday, Nov. 23
Christmas Day	Dec. 25	Monday, Dec. 25

IMPORTANT DATES 2022

July	August	September

October	November	December

IMPORTANT DATES 2023

July	August	September

October	November	December

July	August	September

October	November	December

BIRTHDAYS 2022

July	August	September
-----	-----	-----
-----	-----	-----
-----	-----	-----
-----	-----	-----
-----	-----	-----
-----	-----	-----

October	November	December
-----	-----	-----
-----	-----	-----
-----	-----	-----
-----	-----	-----
-----	-----	-----

BIRTHDAYS 2023

July	August	September

October	November	December

July	August	September

October	November	December

PROJECTS/ GOALS/ NOTES

PROJECTS/ GOALS/ NOTES

JULY 2022

SUNDAY	MONDAY	TUESDAY	WEDNESDAY
○	○	○	○
3	4	5	6
10	11	12	13
17	18	19	20
24	25	26	27
31	○	○	○

THURSDAY	FRIDAY	SATURDAY	GOALS
◯	1	2	
7	8	9	
14	15	16	**NOTES**
21	22	23	
28	29	30	
◯	◯	◯	

JULY 2022

FRIDAY 01
- ○
- ○
- ○
- ○
- ○
- ○

SATURDAY 02
- ○
- ○
- ○
- ○
- ○
- ○

SUNDAY 03
- ○
- ○
- ○
- ○
- ○
- ○

MONDAY 04
- ○
- ○
- ○
- ○
- ○
- ○

TUESDAY 05
- ○
- ○
- ○
- ○
- ○
- ○

WEDNESDAY 06
- ○
- ○
- ○
- ○
- ○
- ○

THURSDAY 07
- ○
- ○
- ○
- ○
- ○
- ○

FRIDAY 08
- ○
- ○
- ○
- ○
- ○
- ○

SATURDAY 09

-
-
-
-
-
-

SUNDAY 10

-
-
-
-
-
-

MONDAY 11

-
-
-
-
-
-

TUESDAY 12

-
-
-
-
-

WEDNESDAY 13

-
-
-
-
-
-

THURSDAY 14

-
-
-
-
-

FRIDAY 15

-
-
-
-
-

SATURDAY 16

-
-
-
-
-

JULY 2022

SUNDAY 17

- ○ --
- ○ --
- ○ --
- ○ --
- ○ --
- ○ --

MONDAY 18

- ○ --
- ○ --
- ○ --
- ○ --
- ○ --
- ○ --

TUESDAY 19

- ○ --
- ○ --
- ○ --
- ○ --
- ○ --
- ○ --

WEDNESDAY 20

- ○ --
- ○ --
- ○ --
- ○ --
- ○ --
- ○ --

THURSDAY 21

- ○ --
- ○ --
- ○ --
- ○ --
- ○ --

FRIDAY 22

- ○ --
- ○ --
- ○ --
- ○ --
- ○ --

SATURDAY 23

- ○ --
- ○ --
- ○ --
- ○ --
- ○ --

SUNDAY 24

- ○ --
- ○ --
- ○ --
- ○ --
- ○ --

MONDAY 25

- ○
- ○
- ○
- ○
- ○
- ○

TUESDAY 26

- ○
- ○
- ○
- ○
- ○
- ○

WEDNESDAY 27

- ○
- ○
- ○
- ○
- ○
- ○

THURSDAY 28

- ○
- ○
- ○
- ○
- ○
- ○

FRIDAY 29

- ○
- ○
- ○
- ○
- ○
- ○

SATURDAY 30

- ○
- ○
- ○
- ○
- ○
- ○

SUNDAY 31

- ○
- ○
- ○
- ○
- ○
- ○

AUGUST 2022

SUNDAY	MONDAY	TUESDAY	WEDNESDAY
○	1	2	3
7	8	9	10
14	15	16	17
21	22	23	24
28	29	30	31
○	○	○	○

THURSDAY	FRIDAY	SATURDAY	GOALS
4	**5**	**6**	
11	**12**	**13**	
18	**19**	**20**	**NOTES**
25	**26**	**27**	
○	○	○	
○	○	○	

AUGUST 2022

MONDAY 01

- ○ --
- ○ --
- ○ --
- ○ --
- ○ --
- ○ --

TUESDAY 02

- ○ --
- ○ --
- ○ --
- ○ --
- ○ --
- ○ --

WEDNESDAY 03

- ○ --
- ○ --
- ○ --
- ○ --
- ○ --
- ○ --

THURSDAY 04

- ○ --
- ○ --
- ○ --
- ○ --
- ○ --
- ○ --

FRIDAY 05

- ○ --
- ○ --
- ○ --
- ○ --
- ○ --
- ○ --

SATURDAY 06

- ○ --
- ○ --
- ○ --
- ○ --
- ○ --
- ○ --

SUNDAY 07

- ○ --
- ○ --
- ○ --
- ○ --
- ○ --
- ○ --

MONDAY 08

- ○ --
- ○ --
- ○ --
- ○ --
- ○ --
- ○ --

TUESDAY 09

○ --
○ --
○ --
○ --
○ --
○ --

WEDNESDAY 10

○ --
○ --
○ --
○ --
○ --
○ --

THURSDAY 11

○ --
○ --
○ --
○ --
○ --
○ --

FRIDAY 12

○ --
○ --
○ --
○ --
○ --
○ --

SATURDAY 13

○ --
○ --
○ --
○ --
○ --
○ --

SUNDAY 14

○ --
○ --
○ --
○ --
○ --
○ --

MONDAY 15

○ --
○ --
○ --
○ --
○ --

TUESDAY 16

○ --
○ --
○ --
○ --
○ --

AUGUST 2022

WEDNESDAY 17

- ○ --
- ○ --
- ○ --
- ○ --
- ○ --
- ○ --

THURSDAY 18

- ○ --
- ○ --
- ○ --
- ○ --
- ○ --
- ○ --

FRIDAY 19

- ○ --
- ○ --
- ○ --
- ○ --
- ○ --
- ○ --

SATURDAY 20

- ○ --
- ○ --
- ○ --
- ○ --
- ○ --
- ○ --

SUNDAY 21

- ○ --
- ○ --
- ○ --
- ○ --
- ○ --
- ○ --

MONDAY 22

- ○ --
- ○ --
- ○ --
- ○ --
- ○ --
- ○ --

TUESDAY 23

- ○ --
- ○ --
- ○ --
- ○ --
- ○ --
- ○ --

WEDNESDAY 24

- ○ --
- ○ --
- ○ --
- ○ --
- ○ --
- ○ --

THURSDAY 25

- ○ --
- ○ --
- ○ --
- ○ --
- ○ --
- ○ --

FRIDAY 26

- ○ --
- ○ --
- ○ --
- ○ --
- ○ --
- ○ --

SATURDAY 27

- ○ --
- ○ --
- ○ --
- ○ --
- ○ --
- ○ --

SUNDAY 28

- ○ --
- ○ --
- ○ --
- ○ --
- ○ --
- ○ --

MONDAY 29

- ○ --
- ○ --
- ○ --
- ○ --
- ○ --
- ○ --

TUESDAY 30

- ○ --
- ○ --
- ○ --
- ○ --
- ○ --
- ○ --

WEDNESDAY 31

- ○ --
- ○ --
- ○ --
- ○ --
- ○ --
- ○ --

SEPTEMBER 2022

SUNDAY	MONDAY	TUESDAY	WEDNESDAY
◯	◯	◯	◯
4	5	6	7
11	12	13	14
18	19	20	21
25	26	27	28
◯	◯	◯	◯

SEPTEMBER 2022

THURSDAY	FRIDAY	SATURDAY
1	2	3
8	9	10
15	16	17
22	23	24
29	30	( )
( )	( )	( )

GOALS

NOTES

SEPTEMBER 2022

THURSDAY 01
- ○ ------------------------------------
- ○ ------------------------------------
- ○ ------------------------------------
- ○ ------------------------------------
- ○ ------------------------------------
- ○ ------------------------------------

FRIDAY 02
- ○ ------------------------------------
- ○ ------------------------------------
- ○ ------------------------------------
- ○ ------------------------------------
- ○ ------------------------------------
- ○ ------------------------------------

SATURDAY 03
- ○ ------------------------------------
- ○ ------------------------------------
- ○ ------------------------------------
- ○ ------------------------------------
- ○ ------------------------------------
- ○ ------------------------------------

SUNDAY 04
- ○ ------------------------------------
- ○ ------------------------------------
- ○ ------------------------------------
- ○ ------------------------------------
- ○ ------------------------------------
- ○ ------------------------------------

MONDAY 05
- ○ ------------------------------------
- ○ ------------------------------------
- ○ ------------------------------------
- ○ ------------------------------------
- ○ ------------------------------------
- ○ ------------------------------------

TUESDAY 06
- ○ ------------------------------------
- ○ ------------------------------------
- ○ ------------------------------------
- ○ ------------------------------------
- ○ ------------------------------------
- ○ ------------------------------------

WEDNESDAY 07
- ○ ------------------------------------
- ○ ------------------------------------
- ○ ------------------------------------
- ○ ------------------------------------
- ○ ------------------------------------
- ○ ------------------------------------

THURSDAY 08
- ○ ------------------------------------
- ○ ------------------------------------
- ○ ------------------------------------
- ○ ------------------------------------
- ○ ------------------------------------
- ○ ------------------------------------

FRIDAY 09

- ○
- ○
- ○
- ○
- ○
- ○

SATURDAY 10

- ○
- ○
- ○
- ○
- ○
- ○

SUNDAY 11

- ○
- ○
- ○
- ○
- ○
- ○

MONDAY 12

- ○
- ○
- ○
- ○
- ○

TUESDAY 13

- ○
- ○
- ○
- ○
- ○
- ○

WEDNESDAY 14

- ○
- ○
- ○
- ○
- ○
- ○

THURSDAY 15

- ○
- ○
- ○
- ○
- ○

FRIDAY 16

- ○
- ○
- ○
- ○
- ○

SEPTEMBER 2022

SATURDAY 17
- ○
- ○
- ○
- ○
- ○
- ○

SUNDAY 18
- ○
- ○
- ○
- ○
- ○
- ○

MONDAY 19
- ○
- ○
- ○
- ○
- ○
- ○

TUESDAY 20
- ○
- ○
- ○
- ○
- ○
- ○

WEDNESDAY 21
- ○
- ○
- ○
- ○
- ○
- ○

THURSDAY 22
- ○
- ○
- ○
- ○
- ○
- ○

FRIDAY 23
- ○
- ○
- ○
- ○
- ○
- ○

SATURDAY 24
- ○
- ○
- ○
- ○
- ○
- ○

SUNDAY 25

-
-
-
-
-
-

MONDAY 26

-
-
-
-
-
-

TUESDAY 27

-
-
-
-
-
-

WEDNESDAY 28

-
-
-
-
-
-

THURSDAY 29

-
-
-
-
-
-

FRIDAY 30

-
-
-
-
-
-

OCTOBER 2022

SUNDAY	MONDAY	TUESDAY	WEDNESDAY
2	3	4	5
9	10	11	12
16	17	18	19
23	24	25	26
30	31		

OCTOBER 2022

THURSDAY	FRIDAY	SATURDAY	GOALS
○	○	1	
6	7	8	
13	14	15	**NOTES**
20	21	22	
27	28	29	
○	○	○	

OCTOBER 2022

SATURDAY 01

- ○ --
- ○ --
- ○ --
- ○ --
- ○ --
- ○ --

SUNDAY 02

- ○ --
- ○ --
- ○ --
- ○ --
- ○ --
- ○ --

MONDAY 03

- ○ --
- ○ --
- ○ --
- ○ --
- ○ --
- ○ --

TUESDAY 04

- ○ --
- ○ --
- ○ --
- ○ --
- ○ --
- ○ --

WEDNESDAY 05

- ○ --
- ○ --
- ○ --
- ○ --
- ○ --
- ○ --

THURSDAY 06

- ○ --
- ○ --
- ○ --
- ○ --
- ○ --
- ○ --

FRIDAY 07

- ○ --
- ○ --
- ○ --
- ○ --
- ○ --
- ○ --

SATURDAY 08

- ○ --
- ○ --
- ○ --
- ○ --
- ○ --
- ○ --

SUNDAY 09

- ○
- ○
- ○
- ○
- ○
- ○

MONDAY 10

- ○
- ○
- ○
- ○
- ○
- ○

TUESDAY 11

- ○
- ○
- ○
- ○
- ○
- ○

WEDNESDAY 12

- ○
- ○
- ○
- ○
- ○

THURSDAY 13

- ○
- ○
- ○
- ○
- ○
- ○

FRIDAY 14

- ○
- ○
- ○
- ○
- ○

SATURDAY 15

- ○
- ○
- ○
- ○
- ○

SUNDAY 16

- ○
- ○
- ○
- ○
- ○

OCTOBER 2022

MONDAY 17

- ○ --
- ○ --
- ○ --
- ○ --
- ○ --
- ○ --

TUESDAY 18

- ○ --
- ○ --
- ○ --
- ○ --
- ○ --
- ○ --

WEDNESDAY 19

- ○ --
- ○ --
- ○ --
- ○ --
- ○ --
- ○ --

THURSDAY 20

- ○ --
- ○ --
- ○ --
- ○ --
- ○ --

FRIDAY 21

- ○ --
- ○ --
- ○ --
- ○ --
- ○ --
- ○ --

SATURDAY 22

- ○ --
- ○ --
- ○ --
- ○ --
- ○ --
- ○ --

SUNDAY 23

- ○ --
- ○ --
- ○ --
- ○ --
- ○ --
- ○ --

MONDAY 24

- ○ --
- ○ --
- ○ --
- ○ --
- ○ --

TUESDAY 25

- ○ --
- ○ --
- ○ --
- ○ --
- ○ --
- ○ --

WEDNESDAY 26

- ○ --
- ○ --
- ○ --
- ○ --
- ○ --
- ○ --

THURSDAY 27

- ○ --
- ○ --
- ○ --
- ○ --
- ○ --
- ○ --

FRIDAY 28

- ○ --
- ○ --
- ○ --
- ○ --
- ○ --
- ○ --

SATURDAY 29

- ○ --
- ○ --
- ○ --
- ○ --
- ○ --
- ○ --

SUNDAY 30

- ○ --
- ○ --
- ○ --
- ○ --
- ○ --
- ○ --

MONDAY 31

- ○ --
- ○ --
- ○ --
- ○ --
- ○ --
- ○ --

NOVEMBER 2022

SUNDAY	MONDAY	TUESDAY	WEDNESDAY
○	○	1	2
6	7	8	9
13	14	15	16
20	21	22	23
27	28	29	30
○	○	○	○

THURSDAY	FRIDAY	SATURDAY	GOALS
3	4	5	
10	11	12	
17	18	19	**NOTES**
24	25	26	

NOVEMBER 2022

TUESDAY 01
- ○ --
- ○ --
- ○ --
- ○ --
- ○ --
- ○ --

WEDNESDAY 02
- ○ --
- ○ --
- ○ --
- ○ --
- ○ --
- ○ --

THURSDAY 03
- ○ --
- ○ --
- ○ --
- ○ --
- ○ --
- ○ --

FRIDAY 04
- ○ --
- ○ --
- ○ --
- ○ --
- ○ --
- ○ --

SATURDAY 05
- ○ --
- ○ --
- ○ --
- ○ --
- ○ --
- ○ --

SUNDAY 06
- ○ --
- ○ --
- ○ --
- ○ --
- ○ --
- ○ --

MONDAY 07
- ○ --
- ○ --
- ○ --
- ○ --
- ○ --
- ○ --

TUESDAY 08
- ○ --
- ○ --
- ○ --
- ○ --
- ○ --
- ○ --

WEDNESDAY 09

- ○ --
- ○ --
- ○ --
- ○ --
- ○ --
- ○ --

THURSDAY 10

- ○ --
- ○ --
- ○ --
- ○ --
- ○ --
- ○ --

FRIDAY 11

- ○ --
- ○ --
- ○ --
- ○ --
- ○ --
- ○ --

SATURDAY 12

- ○ --
- ○ --
- ○ --
- ○ --
- ○ --

SUNDAY 13

- ○ --
- ○ --
- ○ --
- ○ --
- ○ --
- ○ --

MONDAY 14

- ○ --
- ○ --
- ○ --
- ○ --
- ○ --
- ○ --

TUESDAY 15

- ○ --
- ○ --
- ○ --
- ○ --
- ○ --
- ○ --

WEDNESDAY 16

- ○ --
- ○ --
- ○ --
- ○ --
- ○ --

NOVEMBER 2022

THURSDAY 17

- ○ --
- ○ --
- ○ --
- ○ --
- ○ --
- ○ --

FRIDAY 18

- ○ --
- ○ --
- ○ --
- ○ --
- ○ --
- ○ --

SATURDAY 19

- ○ --
- ○ --
- ○ --
- ○ --
- ○ --
- ○ --

SUNDAY 20

- ○ --
- ○ --
- ○ --
- ○ --
- ○ --
- ○ --

MONDAY 21

- ○ --
- ○ --
- ○ --
- ○ --
- ○ --
- ○ --

TUESDAY 22

- ○ --
- ○ --
- ○ --
- ○ --
- ○ --
- ○ --

WEDNESDAY 23

- ○ --
- ○ --
- ○ --
- ○ --
- ○ --

THURSDAY 24

- ○ --
- ○ --
- ○ --
- ○ --
- ○ --

FRIDAY 25

- ○
- ○
- ○
- ○
- ○
- ○

SATURDAY 26

- ○
- ○
- ○
- ○
- ○

SUNDAY 27

- ○
- ○
- ○
- ○
- ○

MONDAY 28

- ○
- ○
- ○
- ○
- ○
- ○

TUESDAY 29

- ○
- ○
- ○
- ○
- ○
- ○

WEDNESDAY 30

- ○
- ○
- ○
- ○
- ○
- ○

DECEMBER 2022

SUNDAY	MONDAY	TUESDAY	WEDNESDAY
◯	◯	◯	◯
4	5	6	7
11	12	13	14
18	19	20	21
25	26	27	28
◯	◯	◯	◯

THURSDAY	FRIDAY	SATURDAY	GOALS
1	2	3	
8	9	10	
15	16	17	**NOTES**
22	23	24	
29	30	31	
○	○	○	

DECEMBER 2022

THURSDAY 01

- ○ --
- ○ --
- ○ --
- ○ --
- ○ --
- ○ --

FRIDAY 02

- ○ --
- ○ --
- ○ --
- ○ --
- ○ --
- ○ --

SATURDAY 03

- ○ --
- ○ --
- ○ --
- ○ --
- ○ --
- ○ --

SUNDAY 04

- ○ --
- ○ --
- ○ --
- ○ --
- ○ --
- ○ --

MONDAY 05

- ○ --
- ○ --
- ○ --
- ○ --
- ○ --
- ○ --

TUESDAY 06

- ○ --
- ○ --
- ○ --
- ○ --
- ○ --
- ○ --

WEDNESDAY 07

- ○ --
- ○ --
- ○ --
- ○ --
- ○ --

THURSDAY 08

- ○ --
- ○ --
- ○ --
- ○ --
- ○ --

FRIDAY 09

- ○ ------------------------------
- ○ ------------------------------
- ○ ------------------------------
- ○ ------------------------------
- ○ ------------------------------
- ○ ------------------------------

SATURDAY 10

- ○ ------------------------------
- ○ ------------------------------
- ○ ------------------------------
- ○ ------------------------------
- ○ ------------------------------

SUNDAY 11

- ○ ------------------------------
- ○ ------------------------------
- ○ ------------------------------
- ○ ------------------------------
- ○ ------------------------------
- ○ ------------------------------

MONDAY 12

- ○ ------------------------------
- ○ ------------------------------
- ○ ------------------------------
- ○ ------------------------------
- ○ ------------------------------
- ○ ------------------------------

TUESDAY 13

- ○ ------------------------------
- ○ ------------------------------
- ○ ------------------------------
- ○ ------------------------------
- ○ ------------------------------
- ○ ------------------------------

WEDNESDAY 14

- ○ ------------------------------
- ○ ------------------------------
- ○ ------------------------------
- ○ ------------------------------
- ○ ------------------------------
- ○ ------------------------------

THURSDAY 15

- ○ ------------------------------
- ○ ------------------------------
- ○ ------------------------------
- ○ ------------------------------
- ○ ------------------------------
- ○ ------------------------------

FRIDAY 16

- ○ ------------------------------
- ○ ------------------------------
- ○ ------------------------------
- ○ ------------------------------
- ○ ------------------------------

DECEMBER 2022

SATURDAY 17

- ○ --
- ○ --
- ○ --
- ○ --
- ○ --
- ○ --

SUNDAY 18

- ○ --
- ○ --
- ○ --
- ○ --
- ○ --
- ○ --

MONDAY 19

- ○ --
- ○ --
- ○ --
- ○ --
- ○ --
- ○ --

TUESDAY 20

- ○ --
- ○ --
- ○ --
- ○ --
- ○ --
- ○ --

WEDNESDAY 21

- ○ --
- ○ --
- ○ --
- ○ --
- ○ --
- ○ --

THURSDAY 22

- ○ --
- ○ --
- ○ --
- ○ --
- ○ --
- ○ --

FRIDAY 23

- ○ --
- ○ --
- ○ --
- ○ --
- ○ --
- ○ --

SATURDAY 24

- ○ --
- ○ --
- ○ --
- ○ --
- ○ --
- ○ --

SUNDAY 25

- ○ ---
- ○ ---
- ○ ---
- ○ ---
- ○ ---
- ○ ---

MONDAY 26

- ○ ---
- ○ ---
- ○ ---
- ○ ---
- ○ ---
- ○ ---

TUESDAY 27

- ○ ---
- ○ ---
- ○ ---
- ○ ---
- ○ ---
- ○ ---

WEDNESDAY 28

- ○ ---
- ○ ---
- ○ ---
- ○ ---
- ○ ---
- ○ ---

THURSDAY 29

- ○ ---
- ○ ---
- ○ ---
- ○ ---
- ○ ---
- ○ ---

FRIDAY 30

- ○ ---
- ○ ---
- ○ ---
- ○ ---
- ○ ---
- ○ ---

SATURDAY 31

- ○ ---
- ○ ---
- ○ ---
- ○ ---
- ○ ---

NOTES

NOTES

NOTES

NOTES

NOTES

NOTES

Happy new year 2023

CONTACTS

Name:

Address:

Phone:

Email:

Name:

Address:

Phone:

Email:

Name:

Address:

Phone:

Email:

Name:

Address:

Phone:

Email:

Name:

Address:

Phone:

Email:

Name:

Address:

Phone:

Email:

Name:

Address:

Phone:

Email:

Name:

Address:

Phone:

Email:

CONTACTS

Name:

Address:

Phone:

Email:

Name:

Address:

Phone:

Email:

Name:

Address:

Phone:

Email:

Name:

Address:

Phone:

Email:

Name:

Address:

Phone:

Email:

Name:

Address:

Phone:

Email:

Name:

Address:

Phone:

Email:

Name:

Address:

Phone:

Email:

PASSWORD LOG

Website: --
Username: --
Password: --
Notes: --

Website: --
Username: --
Password: --
Notes: --

Website: --
Username: --
Password: --
Notes: --

Website: --
Username: --
Password: --
Notes: --

Website: --
Username: --
Password: --
Notes: --

Website: --
Username: --
Password: --
Notes: --

Website: --
Username: --
Password: --
Notes: --

Website: --
Username: --
Password: --
Notes: --

PASSWORD LOG

Website: --------------------------------------

Username: ------------------------------------

Password: ------------------------------------

Notes: --

Website: --------------------------------------

Username: ------------------------------------

Password: ------------------------------------

Notes: --

Website: --------------------------------------

Username: ------------------------------------

Password: ------------------------------------

Notes: --

Website: --------------------------------------

Username: ------------------------------------

Password: ------------------------------------

Notes: --

Website: --------------------------------------

Username: ------------------------------------

Password: ------------------------------------

Notes: --

Website: --------------------------------------

Username: ------------------------------------

Password: ------------------------------------

Notes: --

Website: --------------------------------------

Username: ------------------------------------

Password: ------------------------------------

Notes: --

Website: --------------------------------------

Username: ------------------------------------

Password: ------------------------------------

Notes: --

PROJECTS/ GOALS/ NOTES

PROJECTS/ GOALS/ NOTES

JANUARY 2023

SUNDAY	MONDAY	TUESDAY	WEDNESDAY
1	2	3	4
8	9	10	11
15	16	17	18
22	23	24	25
29	30	31	

THURSDAY	FRIDAY	SATURDAY	GOALS
5	**6**	**7**	
12	**13**	**14**	
19	**20**	**21**	**NOTES**
26	**27**	**28**	
◯	◯	◯	
◯	◯	◯	

JANUARY 2023

SUNDAY 01

- ◯ --
- ◯ --
- ◯ --
- ◯ --
- ◯ --
- ◯ --

MONDAY 02

- ◯ --
- ◯ --
- ◯ --
- ◯ --
- ◯ --
- ◯ --

TUESDAY 03

- ◯ --
- ◯ --
- ◯ --
- ◯ --
- ◯ --
- ◯ --

WEDNESDAY 04

- ◯ --
- ◯ --
- ◯ --
- ◯ --
- ◯ --
- ◯ --

THURSDAY 05

- ◯ --
- ◯ --
- ◯ --
- ◯ --
- ◯ --
- ◯ --

FRIDAY 06

- ◯ --
- ◯ --
- ◯ --
- ◯ --
- ◯ --
- ◯ --

SATURDAY 07

- ◯ --
- ◯ --
- ◯ --
- ◯ --
- ◯ --
- ◯ --

SUNDAY 08

- ◯ --
- ◯ --
- ◯ --
- ◯ --
- ◯ --
- ◯ --

MONDAY 09

- ○ --
- ○ --
- ○ --
- ○ --
- ○ --
- ○ --

TUESDAY 10

- ○ --
- ○ --
- ○ --
- ○ --
- ○ --

WEDNESDAY 11

- ○ --
- ○ --
- ○ --
- ○ --
- ○ --
- ○ --

THURSDAY 12

- ○ --
- ○ --
- ○ --
- ○ --
- ○ --
- ○ --

FRIDAY 13

- ○ --
- ○ --
- ○ --
- ○ --
- ○ --
- ○ --

SATURDAY 14

- ○ --
- ○ --
- ○ --
- ○ --
- ○ --

SUNDAY 15

- ○ --
- ○ --
- ○ --
- ○ --
- ○ --

MONDAY 16

- ○ --
- ○ --
- ○ --
- ○ --
- ○ --

JANUARY 2023

TUESDAY 17

- ○ --
- ○ --
- ○ --
- ○ --
- ○ --
- ○ --

WEDNESDAY 18

- ○ --
- ○ --
- ○ --
- ○ --
- ○ --
- ○ --

THURSDAY 19

- ○ --
- ○ --
- ○ --
- ○ --
- ○ --
- ○ --

FRIDAY 20

- ○ --
- ○ --
- ○ --
- ○ --
- ○ --
- ○ --

SATURDAY 21

- ○ --
- ○ --
- ○ --
- ○ --
- ○ --
- ○ --

SUNDAY 22

- ○ --
- ○ --
- ○ --
- ○ --
- ○ --
- ○ --

MONDAY 23

- ○ --
- ○ --
- ○ --
- ○ --
- ○ --
- ○ --

TUESDAY 24

- ○ --
- ○ --
- ○ --
- ○ --
- ○ --
- ○ --

WEDNESDAY 25

- ○ --
- ○ --
- ○ --
- ○ --
- ○ --
- ○ --

THURSDAY 26

- ○ --
- ○ --
- ○ --
- ○ --
- ○ --
- ○ --

FRIDAY 27

- ○ --
- ○ --
- ○ --
- ○ --
- ○ --
- ○ --

SATURDAY 28

- ○ --
- ○ --
- ○ --
- ○ --
- ○ --
- ○ --

SUNDAY 29

- ○ --
- ○ --
- ○ --
- ○ --
- ○ --
- ○ --

MONDAY 30

- ○ --
- ○ --
- ○ --
- ○ --
- ○ --
- ○ --

TUESDAY 31

- ○ --
- ○ --
- ○ --
- ○ --
- ○ --

FEBRUARY 2023

SUNDAY	MONDAY	TUESDAY	WEDNESDAY
○	○	○	1
5	6	7	8
12	13	14	15
19	20	21	22
26	27	28	○
○	○	○	○

THURSDAY	FRIDAY	SATURDAY	GOALS
(2)	(3)	(4)	
(9)	(10)	(11)	
(16)	(17)	(18)	**NOTES**
(23)	(24)	(25)	
( )	( )	( )	
( )	( )	( )	

FEBRUARY 2023

WEDNESDAY 01

- ○ --
- ○ --
- ○ --
- ○ --
- ○ --
- ○ --

THURSDAY 02

- ○ --
- ○ --
- ○ --
- ○ --
- ○ --
- ○ --

FRIDAY 03

- ○ --
- ○ --
- ○ --
- ○ --
- ○ --
- ○ --

SATURDAY 04

- ○ --
- ○ --
- ○ --
- ○ --
- ○ --

SUNDAY 05

- ○ --
- ○ --
- ○ --
- ○ --
- ○ --
- ○ --

MONDAY 06

- ○ --
- ○ --
- ○ --
- ○ --
- ○ --
- ○ --

TUESDAY 07

- ○ --
- ○ --
- ○ --
- ○ --
- ○ --
- ○ --

WEDNESDAY 08

- ○ --
- ○ --
- ○ --
- ○ --
- ○ --

THURSDAY 09

- ○ --------------------------------
- ○ --------------------------------
- ○ --------------------------------
- ○ --------------------------------
- ○ --------------------------------
- ○ --------------------------------

FRIDAY 10

- ○ --------------------------------
- ○ --------------------------------
- ○ --------------------------------
- ○ --------------------------------
- ○ --------------------------------
- ○ --------------------------------

SATURDAY 11

- ○ --------------------------------
- ○ --------------------------------
- ○ --------------------------------
- ○ --------------------------------
- ○ --------------------------------
- ○ --------------------------------

SUNDAY 12

- ○ --------------------------------
- ○ --------------------------------
- ○ --------------------------------
- ○ --------------------------------
- ○ --------------------------------
- ○ --------------------------------

MONDAY 13

- ○ --------------------------------
- ○ --------------------------------
- ○ --------------------------------
- ○ --------------------------------
- ○ --------------------------------
- ○ --------------------------------

TUESDAY 14

- ○ --------------------------------
- ○ --------------------------------
- ○ --------------------------------
- ○ --------------------------------
- ○ --------------------------------
- ○ --------------------------------

WEDNESDAY 15

- ○ --------------------------------
- ○ --------------------------------
- ○ --------------------------------
- ○ --------------------------------
- ○ --------------------------------
- ○ --------------------------------

THURSDAY 16

- ○ --------------------------------
- ○ --------------------------------
- ○ --------------------------------
- ○ --------------------------------
- ○ --------------------------------
- ○ --------------------------------

FEBRUARY 2023

FRIDAY 17
- ○ --
- ○ --
- ○ --
- ○ --
- ○ --
- ○ --

SATURDAY 18
- ○ --
- ○ --
- ○ --
- ○ --
- ○ --
- ○ --

SUNDAY 19
- ○ --
- ○ --
- ○ --
- ○ --
- ○ --
- ○ --

MONDAY 20
- ○ --
- ○ --
- ○ --
- ○ --
- ○ --
- ○ --

TUESDAY 21
- ○ --
- ○ --
- ○ --
- ○ --
- ○ --
- ○ --

WEDNESDAY 22
- ○ --
- ○ --
- ○ --
- ○ --
- ○ --
- ○ --

THURSDAY 23
- ○ --
- ○ --
- ○ --
- ○ --
- ○ --
- ○ --

FRIDAY 24
- ○ --
- ○ --
- ○ --
- ○ --
- ○ --
- ○ --

SATURDAY 25

○ --

○ --

○ --

○ --

○ --

○ --

SUNDAY 26

○ --

○ --

○ --

○ --

○ --

○ --

MONDAY 27

○ --

○ --

○ --

○ --

○ --

○ --

TUESDAY 28

○ --

○ --

○ --

○ --

○ --

○ --

MARCH 2023

SUNDAY	MONDAY	TUESDAY	WEDNESDAY
○	○	○	1
5	6	7	8
12	13	14	15
19	20	21	22
26	27	28	29
○	○	○	○

THURSDAY	FRIDAY	SATURDAY	GOALS
2	3	4	
9	10	11	
16	17	18	**NOTES**
23	24	25	
30	31	○	
○	○	○	

MARCH 2023

WEDNESDAY 01
- ○ --
- ○ --
- ○ --
- ○ --
- ○ --
- ○ --

THURSDAY 02
- ○ --
- ○ --
- ○ --
- ○ --
- ○ --
- ○ --

FRIDAY 03
- ○ --
- ○ --
- ○ --
- ○ --
- ○ --
- ○ --

SATURDAY 04
- ○ --
- ○ --
- ○ --
- ○ --
- ○ --
- ○ --

SUNDAY 05
- ○ --
- ○ --
- ○ --
- ○ --
- ○ --
- ○ --

MONDAY 06
- ○ --
- ○ --
- ○ --
- ○ --
- ○ --
- ○ --

TUESDAY 07
- ○ --
- ○ --
- ○ --
- ○ --
- ○ --
- ○ --

WEDNESDAY 08
- ○ --
- ○ --
- ○ --
- ○ --
- ○ --
- ○ --

THURSDAY 09

-
-
-
-
-
-

FRIDAY 10

-
-
-
-
-
-

SATURDAY 11

-
-
-
-
-
-

SUNDAY 12

-
-
-
-
-
-

MONDAY 13

-
-
-
-
-
-

TUESDAY 14

-
-
-
-
-
-

WEDNESDAY 15

-
-
-
-
-
-

THURSDAY 16

-
-
-
-
-
-

MARCH 2023

FRIDAY 17

- ○ ---
- ○ ---
- ○ ---
- ○ ---
- ○ ---
- ○ ---

SATURDAY 18

- ○ ---
- ○ ---
- ○ ---
- ○ ---
- ○ ---
- ○ ---

SUNDAY 19

- ○ ---
- ○ ---
- ○ ---
- ○ ---
- ○ ---
- ○ ---

MONDAY 20

- ○ ---
- ○ ---
- ○ ---
- ○ ---
- ○ ---
- ○ ---

TUESDAY 21

- ○ ---
- ○ ---
- ○ ---
- ○ ---
- ○ ---
- ○ ---

WEDNESDAY 22

- ○ ---
- ○ ---
- ○ ---
- ○ ---
- ○ ---
- ○ ---

THURSDAY 23

- ○ ---
- ○ ---
- ○ ---
- ○ ---
- ○ ---
- ○ ---

FRIDAY 24

- ○ ---
- ○ ---
- ○ ---
- ○ ---
- ○ ---
- ○ ---

SATURDAY 25

- ○ ------------------------------
- ○ ------------------------------
- ○ ------------------------------
- ○ ------------------------------
- ○ ------------------------------
- ○ ------------------------------

SUNDAY 26

- ○ ------------------------------
- ○ ------------------------------
- ○ ------------------------------
- ○ ------------------------------
- ○ ------------------------------
- ○ ------------------------------

MONDAY 27

- ○ ------------------------------
- ○ ------------------------------
- ○ ------------------------------
- ○ ------------------------------
- ○ ------------------------------
- ○ ------------------------------

TUESDAY 28

- ○ ------------------------------
- ○ ------------------------------
- ○ ------------------------------
- ○ ------------------------------
- ○ ------------------------------
- ○ ------------------------------

WEDNESDAY 29

- ○ ------------------------------
- ○ ------------------------------
- ○ ------------------------------
- ○ ------------------------------
- ○ ------------------------------
- ○ ------------------------------

THURSDAY 30

- ○ ------------------------------
- ○ ------------------------------
- ○ ------------------------------
- ○ ------------------------------
- ○ ------------------------------
- ○ ------------------------------

FRIDAY 31

- ○ ------------------------------
- ○ ------------------------------
- ○ ------------------------------
- ○ ------------------------------
- ○ ------------------------------

APRIL 2023

SUNDAY	MONDAY	TUESDAY	WEDNESDAY
○	○	○	○
2	3	4	5
9	10	11	12
16	17	18	19
23	24	25	26
30	○	○	○

APRIL 2023

THURSDAY	FRIDAY	SATURDAY	GOALS
○	○	1	
6	7	8	
13	14	15	**NOTES**
20	21	22	
27	28	29	
○	○	○	

APRIL 2023

SATURDAY 01

- ◯ -------------------------------
- ◯ -------------------------------
- ◯ -------------------------------
- ◯ -------------------------------
- ◯ -------------------------------
- ◯ -------------------------------

SUNDAY 02

- ◯ -------------------------------
- ◯ -------------------------------
- ◯ -------------------------------
- ◯ -------------------------------
- ◯ -------------------------------
- ◯ -------------------------------

MONDAY 03

- ◯ -------------------------------
- ◯ -------------------------------
- ◯ -------------------------------
- ◯ -------------------------------
- ◯ -------------------------------
- ◯ -------------------------------

TUESDAY 04

- ◯ -------------------------------
- ◯ -------------------------------
- ◯ -------------------------------
- ◯ -------------------------------
- ◯ -------------------------------

WEDNESDAY 05

- ◯ -------------------------------
- ◯ -------------------------------
- ◯ -------------------------------
- ◯ -------------------------------
- ◯ -------------------------------

THURSDAY 06

- ◯ -------------------------------
- ◯ -------------------------------
- ◯ -------------------------------
- ◯ -------------------------------
- ◯ -------------------------------
- ◯ -------------------------------

FRIDAY 07

- ◯ -------------------------------
- ◯ -------------------------------
- ◯ -------------------------------
- ◯ -------------------------------
- ◯ -------------------------------

SATURDAY 08

- ◯ -------------------------------
- ◯ -------------------------------
- ◯ -------------------------------
- ◯ -------------------------------
- ◯ -------------------------------

SUNDAY 09

- ○ --
- ○ --
- ○ --
- ○ --
- ○ --
- ○ --

MONDAY 10

- ○ --
- ○ --
- ○ --
- ○ --
- ○ --
- ○ --

TUESDAY 11

- ○ --
- ○ --
- ○ --
- ○ --
- ○ --
- ○ --

WEDNESDAY 12

- ○ --
- ○ --
- ○ --
- ○ --
- ○ --

THURSDAY 13

- ○ --
- ○ --
- ○ --
- ○ --
- ○ --
- ○ --

FRIDAY 14

- ○ --
- ○ --
- ○ --
- ○ --
- ○ --
- ○ --

SATURDAY 15

- ○ --
- ○ --
- ○ --
- ○ --
- ○ --

SUNDAY 16

- ○ --
- ○ --
- ○ --
- ○ --
- ○ --

APRIL 2023

MONDAY 17
- ○
- ○
- ○
- ○
- ○
- ○

TUESDAY 18
- ○
- ○
- ○
- ○
- ○
- ○

WEDNESDAY 19
- ○
- ○
- ○
- ○
- ○
- ○

THURSDAY 20
- ○
- ○
- ○
- ○
- ○
- ○

FRIDAY 21
- ○
- ○
- ○
- ○
- ○
- ○

SATURDAY 22
- ○
- ○
- ○
- ○
- ○
- ○

SUNDAY 23
- ○
- ○
- ○
- ○
- ○
- ○

MONDAY 24
- ○
- ○
- ○
- ○
- ○
- ○

TUESDAY 25

- ○ --
- ○ --
- ○ --
- ○ --
- ○ --
- ○ --

WEDNESDAY 26

- ○ --
- ○ --
- ○ --
- ○ --
- ○ --
- ○ --

THURSDAY 27

- ○ --
- ○ --
- ○ --
- ○ --
- ○ --
- ○ --

FRIDAY 28

- ○ --
- ○ --
- ○ --
- ○ --
- ○ --
- ○ --

SATURDAY 29

- ○ --
- ○ --
- ○ --
- ○ --
- ○ --
- ○ --

SUNDAY 30

- ○ --
- ○ --
- ○ --
- ○ --
- ○ --
- ○ --

MAY 2023

SUNDAY	MONDAY	TUESDAY	WEDNESDAY
○	1	2	3
7	8	9	10
14	15	16	17
21	22	23	24
28	29	30	31
○	○	○	○

MAY 2023

THURSDAY	FRIDAY	SATURDAY	GOALS
4	5	6	
11	12	13	
18	19	20	**NOTES**
25	26	27	
( )	( )	( )	
( )	( )	( )	

MAY 2023

MONDAY 01
- ○ --
- ○ --
- ○ --
- ○ --
- ○ --
- ○ --

TUESDAY 02
- ○ --
- ○ --
- ○ --
- ○ --
- ○ --
- ○ --

WEDNESDAY 03
- ○ --
- ○ --
- ○ --
- ○ --
- ○ --
- ○ --

THURSDAY 04
- ○ --
- ○ --
- ○ --
- ○ --
- ○ --
- ○ --

FRIDAY 05
- ○ --
- ○ --
- ○ --
- ○ --
- ○ --
- ○ --

SATURDAY 06
- ○ --
- ○ --
- ○ --
- ○ --
- ○ --
- ○ --

SUNDAY 07
- ○ --
- ○ --
- ○ --
- ○ --
- ○ --
- ○ --

MONDAY 08
- ○ --
- ○ --
- ○ --
- ○ --
- ○ --
- ○ --

TUESDAY 09

○ ------------------------------------
○ ------------------------------------
○ ------------------------------------
○ ------------------------------------
○ ------------------------------------
○ ------------------------------------

WEDNESDAY 10

○ ------------------------------------
○ ------------------------------------
○ ------------------------------------
○ ------------------------------------
○ ------------------------------------
○ ------------------------------------

THURSDAY 11

○ ------------------------------------
○ ------------------------------------
○ ------------------------------------
○ ------------------------------------
○ ------------------------------------
○ ------------------------------------

FRIDAY 12

○ ------------------------------------
○ ------------------------------------
○ ------------------------------------
○ ------------------------------------
○ ------------------------------------
○ ------------------------------------

SATURDAY 13

○ ------------------------------------
○ ------------------------------------
○ ------------------------------------
○ ------------------------------------
○ ------------------------------------
○ ------------------------------------

SUNDAY 14

○ ------------------------------------
○ ------------------------------------
○ ------------------------------------
○ ------------------------------------
○ ------------------------------------
○ ------------------------------------

MONDAY 15

○ ------------------------------------
○ ------------------------------------
○ ------------------------------------
○ ------------------------------------
○ ------------------------------------

TUESDAY 16

○ ------------------------------------
○ ------------------------------------
○ ------------------------------------
○ ------------------------------------
○ ------------------------------------

MAY 2023

WEDNESDAY 17

- ○
- ○
- ○
- ○
- ○
- ○

THURSDAY 18

- ○
- ○
- ○
- ○
- ○
- ○

FRIDAY 19

- ○
- ○
- ○
- ○
- ○
- ○

SATURDAY 20

- ○
- ○
- ○
- ○
- ○
- ○

SUNDAY 21

- ○
- ○
- ○
- ○
- ○
- ○

MONDAY 22

- ○
- ○
- ○
- ○
- ○
- ○

TUESDAY 23

- ○
- ○
- ○
- ○
- ○
- ○

WEDNESDAY 24

- ○
- ○
- ○
- ○
- ○
- ○

THURSDAY 25

- ○ ---------------------------------
- ○ ---------------------------------
- ○ ---------------------------------
- ○ ---------------------------------
- ○ ---------------------------------
- ○ ---------------------------------

FRIDAY 26

- ○ ---------------------------------
- ○ ---------------------------------
- ○ ---------------------------------
- ○ ---------------------------------
- ○ ---------------------------------
- ○ ---------------------------------

SATURDAY 27

- ○ ---------------------------------
- ○ ---------------------------------
- ○ ---------------------------------
- ○ ---------------------------------
- ○ ---------------------------------
- ○ ---------------------------------

SUNDAY 28

- ○ ---------------------------------
- ○ ---------------------------------
- ○ ---------------------------------
- ○ ---------------------------------
- ○ ---------------------------------
- ○ ---------------------------------

MONDAY 29

- ○ ---------------------------------
- ○ ---------------------------------
- ○ ---------------------------------
- ○ ---------------------------------
- ○ ---------------------------------
- ○ ---------------------------------

TUESDAY 30

- ○ ---------------------------------
- ○ ---------------------------------
- ○ ---------------------------------
- ○ ---------------------------------
- ○ ---------------------------------
- ○ ---------------------------------

WEDNESDAY 31

- ○ ---------------------------------
- ○ ---------------------------------
- ○ ---------------------------------
- ○ ---------------------------------
- ○ ---------------------------------
- ○ ---------------------------------

JUNE 2023

SUNDAY	MONDAY	TUESDAY	WEDNESDAY
◯	◯	◯	◯
4	5	6	7
11	12	13	14
18	19	20	21
25	26	27	28
◯	◯	◯	◯

THURSDAY	FRIDAY	SATURDAY	GOALS
1	2	3	
8	9	10	
15	16	17	**NOTES**
22	23	24	
29	30	○	
○	○	○	

JUNE 2023

THURSDAY 01

- ○ --
- ○ --
- ○ --
- ○ --
- ○ --
- ○ --

FRIDAY 02

- ○ --
- ○ --
- ○ --
- ○ --
- ○ --
- ○ --

SATURDAY 03

- ○ --
- ○ --
- ○ --
- ○ --
- ○ --
- ○ --

SUNDAY 04

- ○ --
- ○ --
- ○ --
- ○ --
- ○ --

MONDAY 05

- ○ --
- ○ --
- ○ --
- ○ --
- ○ --
- ○ --

TUESDAY 06

- ○ --
- ○ --
- ○ --
- ○ --
- ○ --
- ○ --

WEDNESDAY 07

- ○ --
- ○ --
- ○ --
- ○ --
- ○ --

THURSDAY 08

- ○ --
- ○ --
- ○ --
- ○ --
- ○ --

FRIDAY 09

- ○ --
- ○ --
- ○ --
- ○ --
- ○ --
- ○ --

SATURDAY 10

- ○ --
- ○ --
- ○ --
- ○ --
- ○ --
- ○ --

SUNDAY 11

- ○ --
- ○ --
- ○ --
- ○ --
- ○ --
- ○ --

MONDAY 12

- ○ --
- ○ --
- ○ --
- ○ --
- ○ --

TUESDAY 13

- ○ --
- ○ --
- ○ --
- ○ --
- ○ --
- ○ --

WEDNESDAY 14

- ○ --
- ○ --
- ○ --
- ○ --
- ○ --
- ○ --

THURSDAY 15

- ○ --
- ○ --
- ○ --
- ○ --
- ○ --

FRIDAY 16

- ○ --
- ○ --
- ○ --
- ○ --
- ○ --

SATURDAY 17

- ○ --
- ○ --
- ○ --
- ○ --
- ○ --
- ○ --

SUNDAY 18

- ○ --
- ○ --
- ○ --
- ○ --
- ○ --
- ○ --

MONDAY 19

- ○ --
- ○ --
- ○ --
- ○ --
- ○ --
- ○ --

TUESDAY 20

- ○ --
- ○ --
- ○ --
- ○ --
- ○ --
- ○ --

WEDNESDAY 21

- ○ --
- ○ --
- ○ --
- ○ --
- ○ --
- ○ --

THURSDAY 22

- ○ --
- ○ --
- ○ --
- ○ --
- ○ --
- ○ --

FRIDAY 23

- ○ --
- ○ --
- ○ --
- ○ --
- ○ --
- ○ --

SATURDAY 24

- ○ --
- ○ --
- ○ --
- ○ --
- ○ --
- ○ --

SUNDAY 25

- ○ --
- ○ --
- ○ --
- ○ --
- ○ --
- ○ --

MONDAY 26

- ○ --
- ○ --
- ○ --
- ○ --
- ○ --
- ○ --

TUESDAY 27

- ○ --
- ○ --
- ○ --
- ○ --
- ○ --
- ○ --

WEDNESDAY 28

- ○ --
- ○ --
- ○ --
- ○ --
- ○ --
- ○ --

THURSDAY 29

- ○ --
- ○ --
- ○ --
- ○ --
- ○ --
- ○ --

FRIDAY 30

- ○ --
- ○ --
- ○ --
- ○ --
- ○ --

JULY 2023

SUNDAY	MONDAY	TUESDAY	WEDNESDAY
○	○	○	○
2	3	4	5
9	10	11	12
16	17	18	19
23	24	25	26
30	31	○	○

THURSDAY	FRIDAY	SATURDAY
○	○	1
6	7	8
13	14	15
20	21	22
27	28	29
○	○	○

GOALS

NOTES

JULY 2023

SATURDAY 01

- ○ --
- ○ --
- ○ --
- ○ --
- ○ --
- ○ --

SUNDAY 02

- ○ --
- ○ --
- ○ --
- ○ --
- ○ --
- ○ --

MONDAY 03

- ○ --
- ○ --
- ○ --
- ○ --
- ○ --
- ○ --

TUESDAY 04

- ○ --
- ○ --
- ○ --
- ○ --
- ○ --
- ○ --

WEDNESDAY 05

- ○ --
- ○ --
- ○ --
- ○ --
- ○ --
- ○ --

THURSDAY 06

- ○ --
- ○ --
- ○ --
- ○ --
- ○ --
- ○ --

FRIDAY 07

- ○ --
- ○ --
- ○ --
- ○ --
- ○ --
- ○ --

SATURDAY 08

- ○ --
- ○ --
- ○ --
- ○ --
- ○ --
- ○ --

SUNDAY 09

○ -------------------------------------
○ -------------------------------------
○ -------------------------------------
○ -------------------------------------
○ -------------------------------------
○ -------------------------------------

MONDAY 10

○ -------------------------------------
○ -------------------------------------
○ -------------------------------------
○ -------------------------------------
○ -------------------------------------
○ -------------------------------------

TUESDAY 11

○ -------------------------------------
○ -------------------------------------
○ -------------------------------------
○ -------------------------------------
○ -------------------------------------
○ -------------------------------------

WEDNESDAY 12

○ -------------------------------------
○ -------------------------------------
○ -------------------------------------
○ -------------------------------------
○ -------------------------------------
○ -------------------------------------

THURSDAY 13

○ -------------------------------------
○ -------------------------------------
○ -------------------------------------
○ -------------------------------------
○ -------------------------------------
○ -------------------------------------

FRIDAY 14

○ -------------------------------------
○ -------------------------------------
○ -------------------------------------
○ -------------------------------------
○ -------------------------------------
○ -------------------------------------

SATURDAY 15

○ -------------------------------------
○ -------------------------------------
○ -------------------------------------
○ -------------------------------------
○ -------------------------------------

SUNDAY 16

○ -------------------------------------
○ -------------------------------------
○ -------------------------------------
○ -------------------------------------
○ -------------------------------------

JULY 2023

MONDAY 17

- ○ --
- ○ --
- ○ --
- ○ --
- ○ --
- ○ --

TUESDAY 18

- ○ --
- ○ --
- ○ --
- ○ --
- ○ --
- ○ --

WEDNESDAY 19

- ○ --
- ○ --
- ○ --
- ○ --
- ○ --
- ○ --

THURSDAY 20

- ○ --
- ○ --
- ○ --
- ○ --
- ○ --

FRIDAY 21

- ○ --
- ○ --
- ○ --
- ○ --
- ○ --
- ○ --

SATURDAY 22

- ○ --
- ○ --
- ○ --
- ○ --
- ○ --
- ○ --

SUNDAY 23

- ○ --
- ○ --
- ○ --
- ○ --
- ○ --

MONDAY 24

- ○ --
- ○ --
- ○ --
- ○ --
- ○ --

TUESDAY 25

- ○ ---
- ○ ---
- ○ ---
- ○ ---
- ○ ---
- ○ ---

WEDNESDAY 26

- ○ ---
- ○ ---
- ○ ---
- ○ ---
- ○ ---
- ○ ---

THURSDAY 27

- ○ ---
- ○ ---
- ○ ---
- ○ ---
- ○ ---
- ○ ---

FRIDAY 28

- ○ ---
- ○ ---
- ○ ---
- ○ ---
- ○ ---

SATURDAY 29

- ○ ---
- ○ ---
- ○ ---
- ○ ---
- ○ ---
- ○ ---

SUNDAY 30

- ○ ---
- ○ ---
- ○ ---
- ○ ---
- ○ ---
- ○ ---

MONDAY 31

- ○ ---
- ○ ---
- ○ ---
- ○ ---
- ○ ---
- ○ ---

AUGUST 2023

SUNDAY	MONDAY	TUESDAY	WEDNESDAY
○	○	1	2
6	7	8	9
13	14	15	16
20	21	22	23
27	28	29	30
○	○	○	○

THURSDAY	FRIDAY	SATURDAY	GOALS
(3)	(4)	(5)	
(10)	(11)	(12)	
(17)	(18)	(19)	**NOTES**
(24)	(25)	(26)	
(31)	( )	( )	
( )	( )	( )	

AUGUST 2023

TUESDAY 01

- ○ ------------------------------------
- ○ ------------------------------------
- ○ ------------------------------------
- ○ ------------------------------------
- ○ ------------------------------------
- ○ ------------------------------------

WEDNESDAY 02

- ○ ------------------------------------
- ○ ------------------------------------
- ○ ------------------------------------
- ○ ------------------------------------
- ○ ------------------------------------
- ○ ------------------------------------

THURSDAY 03

- ○ ------------------------------------
- ○ ------------------------------------
- ○ ------------------------------------
- ○ ------------------------------------
- ○ ------------------------------------
- ○ ------------------------------------

FRIDAY 04

- ○ ------------------------------------
- ○ ------------------------------------
- ○ ------------------------------------
- ○ ------------------------------------
- ○ ------------------------------------
- ○ ------------------------------------

SATURDAY 05

- ○ ------------------------------------
- ○ ------------------------------------
- ○ ------------------------------------
- ○ ------------------------------------
- ○ ------------------------------------
- ○ ------------------------------------

SUNDAY 06

- ○ ------------------------------------
- ○ ------------------------------------
- ○ ------------------------------------
- ○ ------------------------------------
- ○ ------------------------------------
- ○ ------------------------------------

MONDAY 07

- ○ ------------------------------------
- ○ ------------------------------------
- ○ ------------------------------------
- ○ ------------------------------------
- ○ ------------------------------------

TUESDAY 08

- ○ ------------------------------------
- ○ ------------------------------------
- ○ ------------------------------------
- ○ ------------------------------------
- ○ ------------------------------------

WEDNESDAY 09

- ○ ----------------------------------
- ○ ----------------------------------
- ○ ----------------------------------
- ○ ----------------------------------
- ○ ----------------------------------
- ○ ----------------------------------

THURSDAY 10

- ○ ----------------------------------
- ○ ----------------------------------
- ○ ----------------------------------
- ○ ----------------------------------
- ○ ----------------------------------
- ○ ----------------------------------

FRIDAY 11

- ○ ----------------------------------
- ○ ----------------------------------
- ○ ----------------------------------
- ○ ----------------------------------
- ○ ----------------------------------
- ○ ----------------------------------

SATURDAY 12

- ○ ----------------------------------
- ○ ----------------------------------
- ○ ----------------------------------
- ○ ----------------------------------
- ○ ----------------------------------

SUNDAY 13

- ○ ----------------------------------
- ○ ----------------------------------
- ○ ----------------------------------
- ○ ----------------------------------
- ○ ----------------------------------
- ○ ----------------------------------

MONDAY 14

- ○ ----------------------------------
- ○ ----------------------------------
- ○ ----------------------------------
- ○ ----------------------------------
- ○ ----------------------------------
- ○ ----------------------------------

TUESDAY 15

- ○ ----------------------------------
- ○ ----------------------------------
- ○ ----------------------------------
- ○ ----------------------------------
- ○ ----------------------------------

WEDNESDAY 16

- ○ ----------------------------------
- ○ ----------------------------------
- ○ ----------------------------------
- ○ ----------------------------------
- ○ ----------------------------------

AUGUST 2023

THURSDAY 17

- ○ --
- ○ --
- ○ --
- ○ --
- ○ --
- ○ --

FRIDAY 18

- ○ --
- ○ --
- ○ --
- ○ --
- ○ --
- ○ --

SATURDAY 19

- ○ --
- ○ --
- ○ --
- ○ --
- ○ --
- ○ --

SUNDAY 20

- ○ --
- ○ --
- ○ --
- ○ --
- ○ --
- ○ --

MONDAY 21

- ○ --
- ○ --
- ○ --
- ○ --
- ○ --
- ○ --

TUESDAY 22

- ○ --
- ○ --
- ○ --
- ○ --
- ○ --
- ○ --

WEDNESDAY 23

- ○ --
- ○ --
- ○ --
- ○ --
- ○ --
- ○ --

THURSDAY 24

- ○ --
- ○ --
- ○ --
- ○ --
- ○ --
- ○ --

FRIDAY 25

- ○
- ○
- ○
- ○
- ○
- ○

SATURDAY 26

- ○
- ○
- ○
- ○
- ○
- ○

SUNDAY 27

- ○
- ○
- ○
- ○
- ○
- ○

MONDAY 28

- ○
- ○
- ○
- ○
- ○
- ○

TUESDAY 29

- ○
- ○
- ○
- ○
- ○
- ○

WEDNESDAY 30

- ○
- ○
- ○
- ○
- ○
- ○

THURSDAY 31

- ○
- ○
- ○
- ○
- ○
- ○

SEPTEMBER 2023

SUNDAY	MONDAY	TUESDAY	WEDNESDAY
◯	◯	◯	◯
3	4	5	6
10	11	12	13
17	18	19	20
24	25	26	27
◯	◯	◯	◯

THURSDAY	FRIDAY	SATURDAY	GOALS
◯	1	2	
7	8	9	
14	15	16	**NOTES**
21	22	23	
28	29	30	
◯	◯	◯	

SEPTEMBER 2023

FRIDAY 01

- ○ --
- ○ --
- ○ --
- ○ --
- ○ --
- ○ --

SATURDAY 02

- ○ --
- ○ --
- ○ --
- ○ --
- ○ --
- ○ --

SUNDAY 03

- ○ --
- ○ --
- ○ --
- ○ --
- ○ --
- ○ --

MONDAY 04

- ○ --
- ○ --
- ○ --
- ○ --
- ○ --
- ○ --

TUESDAY 05

- ○ --
- ○ --
- ○ --
- ○ --
- ○ --
- ○ --

WEDNESDAY 06

- ○ --
- ○ --
- ○ --
- ○ --
- ○ --
- ○ --

THURSDAY 07

- ○ --
- ○ --
- ○ --
- ○ --
- ○ --

FRIDAY 08

- ○ --
- ○ --
- ○ --
- ○ --
- ○ --

SATURDAY 09

- ○ --
- ○ --
- ○ --
- ○ --
- ○ --
- ○ --

SUNDAY 10

- ○ --
- ○ --
- ○ --
- ○ --
- ○ --

MONDAY 11

- ○ --
- ○ --
- ○ --
- ○ --
- ○ --
- ○ --

TUESDAY 12

- ○ --
- ○ --
- ○ --
- ○ --
- ○ --

WEDNESDAY 13

- ○ --
- ○ --
- ○ --
- ○ --
- ○ --
- ○ --

THURSDAY 14

- ○ --
- ○ --
- ○ --
- ○ --
- ○ --

FRIDAY 15

- ○ --
- ○ --
- ○ --
- ○ --
- ○ --

SATURDAY 16

- ○ --
- ○ --
- ○ --
- ○ --
- ○ --

SEPTEMBER 2023

SUNDAY 17

- ○ --
- ○ --
- ○ --
- ○ --
- ○ --
- ○ --

MONDAY 18

- ○ --
- ○ --
- ○ --
- ○ --
- ○ --
- ○ --

TUESDAY 19

- ○ --
- ○ --
- ○ --
- ○ --
- ○ --
- ○ --

WEDNESDAY 20

- ○ --
- ○ --
- ○ --
- ○ --
- ○ --
- ○ --

THURSDAY 21

- ○ --
- ○ --
- ○ --
- ○ --
- ○ --
- ○ --

FRIDAY 22

- ○ --
- ○ --
- ○ --
- ○ --
- ○ --
- ○ --

SATURDAY 23

- ○ --
- ○ --
- ○ --
- ○ --
- ○ --
- ○ --

SUNDAY 24

- ○ --
- ○ --
- ○ --
- ○ --
- ○ --
- ○ --

MONDAY 25

○ --------------------------------------
○ --------------------------------------
○ --------------------------------------
○ --------------------------------------
○ --------------------------------------
○ --------------------------------------

TUESDAY 26

○ --------------------------------------
○ --------------------------------------
○ --------------------------------------
○ --------------------------------------
○ --------------------------------------
○ --------------------------------------

WEDNESDAY 27

○ --------------------------------------
○ --------------------------------------
○ --------------------------------------
○ --------------------------------------
○ --------------------------------------
○ --------------------------------------

THURSDAY 28

○ --------------------------------------
○ --------------------------------------
○ --------------------------------------
○ --------------------------------------
○ --------------------------------------

FRIDAY 29

○ --------------------------------------
○ --------------------------------------
○ --------------------------------------
○ --------------------------------------
○ --------------------------------------
○ --------------------------------------

SATURDAY 30

○ --------------------------------------
○ --------------------------------------
○ --------------------------------------
○ --------------------------------------
○ --------------------------------------

OCTOBER 2023

SUNDAY	MONDAY	TUESDAY	WEDNESDAY
1	2	3	4
8	9	10	11
15	16	17	18
22	23	24	25
29	30	31	

THURSDAY	FRIDAY	SATURDAY
5	6	7
12	13	14
19	20	21
26	27	28
◯	◯	◯
◯	◯	◯

GOALS

NOTES

OCTOBER 2023

SUNDAY 01

- ○ -------------------------------------
- ○ -------------------------------------
- ○ -------------------------------------
- ○ -------------------------------------
- ○ -------------------------------------
- ○ -------------------------------------

MONDAY 02

- ○ -------------------------------------
- ○ -------------------------------------
- ○ -------------------------------------
- ○ -------------------------------------
- ○ -------------------------------------
- ○ -------------------------------------

TUESDAY 03

- ○ -------------------------------------
- ○ -------------------------------------
- ○ -------------------------------------
- ○ -------------------------------------
- ○ -------------------------------------
- ○ -------------------------------------

WEDNESDAY 04

- ○ -------------------------------------
- ○ -------------------------------------
- ○ -------------------------------------
- ○ -------------------------------------
- ○ -------------------------------------
- ○ -------------------------------------

THURSDAY 05

- ○ -------------------------------------
- ○ -------------------------------------
- ○ -------------------------------------
- ○ -------------------------------------
- ○ -------------------------------------
- ○ -------------------------------------

FRIDAY 06

- ○ -------------------------------------
- ○ -------------------------------------
- ○ -------------------------------------
- ○ -------------------------------------
- ○ -------------------------------------
- ○ -------------------------------------

SATURDAY 07

- ○ -------------------------------------
- ○ -------------------------------------
- ○ -------------------------------------
- ○ -------------------------------------
- ○ -------------------------------------
- ○ -------------------------------------

SUNDAY 08

- ○ -------------------------------------
- ○ -------------------------------------
- ○ -------------------------------------
- ○ -------------------------------------
- ○ -------------------------------------

MONDAY 09

- ○ -----------------------------------
- ○ -----------------------------------
- ○ -----------------------------------
- ○ -----------------------------------
- ○ -----------------------------------
- ○ -----------------------------------

TUESDAY 10

- ○ -----------------------------------
- ○ -----------------------------------
- ○ -----------------------------------
- ○ -----------------------------------
- ○ -----------------------------------
- ○ -----------------------------------

WEDNESDAY 11

- ○ -----------------------------------
- ○ -----------------------------------
- ○ -----------------------------------
- ○ -----------------------------------
- ○ -----------------------------------
- ○ -----------------------------------

THURSDAY 12

- ○ -----------------------------------
- ○ -----------------------------------
- ○ -----------------------------------
- ○ -----------------------------------
- ○ -----------------------------------

FRIDAY 13

- ○ -----------------------------------
- ○ -----------------------------------
- ○ -----------------------------------
- ○ -----------------------------------
- ○ -----------------------------------
- ○ -----------------------------------

SATURDAY 14

- ○ -----------------------------------
- ○ -----------------------------------
- ○ -----------------------------------
- ○ -----------------------------------
- ○ -----------------------------------
- ○ -----------------------------------

SUNDAY 15

- ○ -----------------------------------
- ○ -----------------------------------
- ○ -----------------------------------
- ○ -----------------------------------
- ○ -----------------------------------
- ○ -----------------------------------

MONDAY 16

- ○ -----------------------------------
- ○ -----------------------------------
- ○ -----------------------------------
- ○ -----------------------------------
- ○ -----------------------------------

OCTOBER 2023

TUESDAY 17

- ○
- ○
- ○
- ○
- ○
- ○

WEDNESDAY 18

- ○
- ○
- ○
- ○
- ○
- ○

THURSDAY 19

- ○
- ○
- ○
- ○
- ○
- ○

FRIDAY 20

- ○
- ○
- ○
- ○
- ○
- ○

SATURDAY 21

- ○
- ○
- ○
- ○
- ○
- ○

SUNDAY 22

- ○
- ○
- ○
- ○
- ○
- ○

MONDAY 23

- ○
- ○
- ○
- ○
- ○
- ○

TUESDAY 24

- ○
- ○
- ○
- ○
- ○
- ○

WEDNESDAY 25

- ○ --
- ○ --
- ○ --
- ○ --
- ○ --
- ○ --

THURSDAY 26

- ○ --
- ○ --
- ○ --
- ○ --
- ○ --
- ○ --

FRIDAY 27

- ○ --
- ○ --
- ○ --
- ○ --
- ○ --
- ○ --

SATURDAY 28

- ○ --
- ○ --
- ○ --
- ○ --
- ○ --
- ○ --

SUNDAY 29

- ○ --
- ○ --
- ○ --
- ○ --
- ○ --
- ○ --

MONDAY 30

- ○ --
- ○ --
- ○ --
- ○ --
- ○ --
- ○ --

TUESDAY 31

- ○ --
- ○ --
- ○ --
- ○ --
- ○ --
- ○ --

NOVEMBER 2023

SUNDAY	MONDAY	TUESDAY	WEDNESDAY
◯	◯	◯	1
5	6	7	8
12	13	14	15
19	20	21	22
26	27	28	29
◯	◯	◯	◯

THURSDAY	FRIDAY	SATURDAY	GOALS
2	**3**	**4**	
9	**10**	**11**	
16	**17**	**18**	**NOTES**
23	**24**	**25**	
30	◯	◯	
◯	◯	◯	

NOVEMBER 2023

WEDNESDAY 01

- ○ ----------------------------
- ○ ----------------------------
- ○ ----------------------------
- ○ ----------------------------
- ○ ----------------------------
- ○ ----------------------------

THURSDAY 02

- ○ ----------------------------
- ○ ----------------------------
- ○ ----------------------------
- ○ ----------------------------
- ○ ----------------------------
- ○ ----------------------------

FRIDAY 03

- ○ ----------------------------
- ○ ----------------------------
- ○ ----------------------------
- ○ ----------------------------
- ○ ----------------------------
- ○ ----------------------------

SATURDAY 04

- ○ ----------------------------
- ○ ----------------------------
- ○ ----------------------------
- ○ ----------------------------
- ○ ----------------------------
- ○ ----------------------------

SUNDAY 05

- ○ ----------------------------
- ○ ----------------------------
- ○ ----------------------------
- ○ ----------------------------
- ○ ----------------------------
- ○ ----------------------------

MONDAY 06

- ○ ----------------------------
- ○ ----------------------------
- ○ ----------------------------
- ○ ----------------------------
- ○ ----------------------------
- ○ ----------------------------

TUESDAY 07

- ○ ----------------------------
- ○ ----------------------------
- ○ ----------------------------
- ○ ----------------------------
- ○ ----------------------------
- ○ ----------------------------

WEDNESDAY 08

- ○ ----------------------------
- ○ ----------------------------
- ○ ----------------------------
- ○ ----------------------------
- ○ ----------------------------
- ○ ----------------------------

THURSDAY 09

- ○ --
- ○ --
- ○ --
- ○ --
- ○ --
- ○ --

FRIDAY 10

- ○ --
- ○ --
- ○ --
- ○ --
- ○ --
- ○ --

SATURDAY 11

- ○ --
- ○ --
- ○ --
- ○ --
- ○ --
- ○ --

SUNDAY 12

- ○ --
- ○ --
- ○ --
- ○ --
- ○ --
- ○ --

MONDAY 13

- ○ --
- ○ --
- ○ --
- ○ --
- ○ --
- ○ --

TUESDAY 14

- ○ --
- ○ --
- ○ --
- ○ --
- ○ --
- ○ --

WEDNESDAY 15

- ○ --
- ○ --
- ○ --
- ○ --
- ○ --
- ○ --

THURSDAY 16

- ○ --
- ○ --
- ○ --
- ○ --
- ○ --
- ○ --

NOVEMBER 2023

FRIDAY 17

- ○ -----
- ○ -----
- ○ -----
- ○ -----
- ○ -----
- ○ -----

SATURDAY 18

- ○ -----
- ○ -----
- ○ -----
- ○ -----
- ○ -----
- ○ -----

SUNDAY 19

- ○ -----
- ○ -----
- ○ -----
- ○ -----
- ○ -----
- ○ -----

MONDAY 20

- ○ -----
- ○ -----
- ○ -----
- ○ -----
- ○ -----
- ○ -----

TUESDAY 21

- ○ -----
- ○ -----
- ○ -----
- ○ -----
- ○ -----

WEDNESDAY 22

- ○ -----
- ○ -----
- ○ -----
- ○ -----
- ○ -----
- ○ -----

THURSDAY 23

- ○ -----
- ○ -----
- ○ -----
- ○ -----
- ○ -----
- ○ -----

FRIDAY 24

- ○ -----
- ○ -----
- ○ -----
- ○ -----
- ○ -----
- ○ -----

SATURDAY 25

○ --
○ --
○ --
○ --
○ --
○ --

SUNDAY 26

○ --
○ --
○ --
○ --
○ --
○ --

MONDAY 27

○ --
○ --
○ --
○ --
○ --
○ --

TUESDAY 28

○ --
○ --
○ --
○ --
○ --
○ --

WEDNESDAY 29

○ --
○ --
○ --
○ --
○ --
○ --

THURSDAY 30

○ --
○ --
○ --
○ --
○ --

DECEMBER 2023

SUNDAY	MONDAY	TUESDAY	WEDNESDAY
◯	◯	◯	◯
3	4	5	6
10	11	12	13
17	18	19	20
24	25	26	27
31	◯	◯	◯

DECEMBER 2023

THURSDAY	FRIDAY	SATURDAY	GOALS
○	1	2	
7	8	9	
14	15	16	**NOTES**
21	22	23	
28	29	30	
○	○	○	

DECEMBER 2023

FRIDAY 01
- ○ --
- ○ --
- ○ --
- ○ --
- ○ --
- ○ --

SATURDAY 02
- ○ --
- ○ --
- ○ --
- ○ --
- ○ --
- ○ --

SUNDAY 03
- ○ --
- ○ --
- ○ --
- ○ --
- ○ --
- ○ --

MONDAY 04
- ○ --
- ○ --
- ○ --
- ○ --
- ○ --

TUESDAY 05
- ○ --
- ○ --
- ○ --
- ○ --
- ○ --
- ○ --

WEDNESDAY 06
- ○ --
- ○ --
- ○ --
- ○ --
- ○ --
- ○ --

THURSDAY 07
- ○ --
- ○ --
- ○ --
- ○ --
- ○ --
- ○ --

FRIDAY 08
- ○ --
- ○ --
- ○ --
- ○ --
- ○ --

SATURDAY 09

- ○
- ○
- ○
- ○
- ○
- ○

SUNDAY 10

- ○
- ○
- ○
- ○
- ○
- ○

MONDAY 11

- ○
- ○
- ○
- ○
- ○
- ○

TUESDAY 12

- ○
- ○
- ○
- ○
- ○

WEDNESDAY 13

- ○
- ○
- ○
- ○
- ○
- ○

THURSDAY 14

- ○
- ○
- ○
- ○
- ○
- ○

FRIDAY 15

- ○
- ○
- ○
- ○
- ○

SATURDAY 16

- ○
- ○
- ○
- ○
- ○

DECEMBER 2023

SUNDAY 17

- ○
- ○
- ○
- ○
- ○
- ○

MONDAY 18

- ○
- ○
- ○
- ○
- ○
- ○

TUESDAY 19

- ○
- ○
- ○
- ○
- ○
- ○

WEDNESDAY 20

- ○
- ○
- ○
- ○
- ○
- ○

THURSDAY 21

- ○
- ○
- ○
- ○
- ○

FRIDAY 22

- ○
- ○
- ○
- ○
- ○

SATURDAY 23

- ○
- ○
- ○
- ○
- ○

SUNDAY 24

- ○
- ○
- ○
- ○
- ○

MONDAY 25

○ --
○ --
○ --
○ --
○ --
○ --

TUESDAY 26

○ --
○ --
○ --
○ --
○ --
○ --

WEDNESDAY 27

○ --
○ --
○ --
○ --
○ --
○ --

THURSDAY 28

○ --
○ --
○ --
○ --
○ --
○ --

FRIDAY 29

○ --
○ --
○ --
○ --
○ --
○ --

SATURDAY 30

○ --
○ --
○ --
○ --
○ --
○ --

SUNDAY 31

○ --
○ --
○ --
○ --
○ --

NOTES

NOTES

NOTES

NOTES

NOTES

NOTES

NOTES

NOTES

PASSWORD LOG

Website: --
Username: --
Password: --
Notes: --

Website: --
Username: --
Password: --
Notes: --

Website: --
Username: --
Password: --
Notes: --

Website: --
Username: --
Password: --
Notes: --

Website: --
Username: --
Password: --
Notes: --

Website: --
Username: --
Password: --
Notes: --

Website: --
Username: --
Password: --
Notes: --

Website: --
Username: --
Password: --
Notes: --

PASSWORD LOG

Website: --

Username: ---------------------------------------

Password: ---------------------------------------

Notes: --

Website: --

Username: ---------------------------------------

Password: ---------------------------------------

Notes: --

Website: --

Username: ---------------------------------------

Password: ---------------------------------------

Notes: --

Website: --

Username: ---------------------------------------

Password: ---------------------------------------

Notes: --

Website: --

Username: ---------------------------------------

Password: ---------------------------------------

Notes: --

Website: --

Username: ---------------------------------------

Password: ---------------------------------------

Notes: --

Website: --

Username: ---------------------------------------

Password: ---------------------------------------

Notes: --

Website: --

Username: ---------------------------------------

Password: ---------------------------------------

Notes: --

PASSWORD LOG

Website: ----------------------------------

Username: -------------------------------

Password: -------------------------------

Notes: -------------------------------------

Website: ----------------------------------

Username: -------------------------------

Password: -------------------------------

Notes: -------------------------------------

Website: ----------------------------------

Username: -------------------------------

Password: -------------------------------

Notes: -------------------------------------

Website: ----------------------------------

Username: -------------------------------

Password: -------------------------------

Notes: -------------------------------------

Website: ----------------------------------

Username: -------------------------------

Password: -------------------------------

Notes: -------------------------------------

Website: ----------------------------------

Username: -------------------------------

Password: -------------------------------

Notes: -------------------------------------

Website: ----------------------------------

Username: -------------------------------

Password: -------------------------------

Notes: -------------------------------------

Website: ----------------------------------

Username: -------------------------------

Password: -------------------------------

Notes: -------------------------------------

PASSWORD LOG

Website: --

Username: --

Password: --

Notes: --

Website: --

Username: --

Password: --

Notes: --

Website: --

Username: --

Password: --

Notes: --

Website: --

Username: --

Password: --

Notes: --

Website: --

Username: --

Password: --

Notes: --

Website: --

Username: --

Password: --

Notes: --

Website: --

Username: --

Password: --

Notes: --

Website: --

Username: --

Password: --

Notes: --

Made in the USA
Monee, IL
23 September 2022

14295436R00083